Scholastic
daily
planner

NAME _____

SCHOOL _____

LEVEL _____

YEAR _____

EMERGENCY PHONE NUMBERS

Police _____ **Doctor** _____ **Fire** _____

SCHEDULE

TIME	Monday	Tuesday	Wednesday	Thursday	Fri

SCHEDULE

TIME	Monday	Tuesday	Wednesday	Thursday	Frid

SCHEDULE

	Monday	Tuesday	Wednesday	Thursday	Friday

SCHEDULE

	Monday	Tuesday	Wednesday	Thursday	Friday

CLASS RECORD

Pupil Name/Number	Telephone No.	Address

CLASS RECORD

Pupil Name/Number	Telephone No.	Address

SPECIAL GROUPS
(Reading and other subjects; activities)

Pupils

Materials

Pupils

Materials

Other

SEATING CHARTS

SCHOOL CALENDAR

Important Days in the School Year

begins _____

ay—1st Monday in September

hip Day—September 17

ppur—in Sept. or Oct.

ashanah—in Sept. or Oct.

us Day—2nd Monday in Oct.

an Thanksgiving—2nd Monday in Oct.

vention Week—in October

Nations Day—October 24

en—October 31

's Book Week—in November

Education Week—in November

s Day—November 11

giving Day—4th Thursday in Nov.

Rights Day—December 10

ights Day—December 15

ah—November or December

as—December 25

ns _____

ar's Day—January 1

uther King's birthday—Jan. 15

E. Lee's birthday—January 19

Black History Month—February

Dental Health Week—in February

Groundhog Day—February 2

Lincoln's birthday—February 12

Valentine's Day—February 14

Washington's birthday—February 22

Presidents' Day—3rd Monday in Feb.

Canadian Heritage Day—3rd Monday
in Feb.

St. Patrick's Day—March 17

Easter—March or April

Passover—March or April

April Fool's Day—April 1

Arbor Day—around April 22

Mother's Day—2nd Sunday in May

Victoria Day—Monday before May 25

Memorial Day—May 30

Father's Day—3rd Sunday in June

Flag Day—June 14

Canada Day—July 1

Independence Day—July 4

School closes _____

These are usual dates. Check annually for any changes.

GRADING PERIODS

	Begins	Issued
1st Term	_____	Report _____
2nd Term	_____	Report _____
3rd Term	_____	Report _____
4th Term	_____	Report _____
5th Term	_____	Report _____
6th Term	_____	Report _____
7th Term	_____	Report _____
8th Term	_____	Report _____
9th Term	_____	Report _____
10th Term	_____	Report _____

DAYS TO REMEMBER

Week of _____   Lunchroom _____   Playground _____

Date ___ **Monday**			
Date ___ **Tuesday**			
Date ___ **Wednesday**			
Date ___ **Thursday**			
Date ___ **Friday**			

Education does not commence with the alphabet; it begins with handfuls of flowers in green dells, with birds' nests admired; with creeping ants, and almost imperceptible emmets; with pleasant walks in shady lanes, and with thoughts directed in sweet and kindly tones and words to nature, to acts of benevolence and virtue.   Anonymous

Week of _____   Lunchroom _____   Playground _____

Date ____ **Monday**			
Date ____ **Tuesday**			
Date ____ **Wednesday**			
Date ____ **Thursday**			
Date ____ **Friday**			

Special Events _____   Meetings _____

The mediocre teacher tells. The good teacher explains. The superior teacher demonstrates. The great teacher inspires.

William Arthur Ward

Week of _____   Lunchroom _____   Playground _____

Date ___ **Monday**			
Date ___ **Tuesday**			
Date ___ **Wednesday**			
Date ___ **Thursday**			
Date ___ **Friday**			

Special Events _____   Meetings _____

What office is there which involves
more responsibility, which requires
more qualifications, and which ought,
therefore, to be more honorable, than
that of teaching?   Harriet Martineau

Week of _____   Lunchroom _____   Playground _____

Date _____ **Monday**			
Date _____ **Tuesday**			
Date _____ **Wednesday**			
Date _____ **Thursday**			
Date _____ **Friday**			

We must have a place where children can have a whole group of adults they can trust.   Margaret Mead

Week of _____   Lunchroom _____   Playground _____

Date ___ **Monday**			
Date ___ **Tuesday**			
Date ___ **Wednesday**			
Date ___ **Thursday**			
Date ___ **Friday**			

Special Events _____   Meetings _____

Educators should be chosen not merely for their special qualifications, but more for their personality and character, because we teach more by what we are than by what we teach.   Will Durant

Week of _____ Lunchroom _____ Playground _____

Date ____ **Monday**			
Date ____ **Tuesday**			
Date ____ **Wednesday**			
Date ____ **Thursday**			
Date ____ **Friday**			

Special Events _____   Meetings _____

Teachers teach because they care.
Teaching young people is what they
do best. It requires long hours,
patience, and care.   Horace Mann

Week of _____ Lunchroom _____ Playground _____

Date ___ **Monday**			
Date ___ **Tuesday**			
Date ___ **Wednesday**			
Date ___ **Thursday**			
Date ___ **Friday**			

Special Events _____   Meetings _____

It is like what we imagine knowledge to be:
dark, salt, clear, moving, utterly free,
drawn from the cold hard mouth of the
word. . .   Elizabeth Bishop

Date ___ **Monday**			
Date ___ **Tuesday**			
Date ___ **Wednesday**			
Date ___ **Thursday**			
Date ___ **Friday**			

Special Events _____   Meetings _____

			In all our efforts for education—in providing adequate school research, and study—we must never lose sight of the very heart of education: good teaching itself. Good teachers do not just happen, they are the product of the highest of personal motivation. Dwight D. Eisenhower

Week of _____   Lunchroom _____   Playground _____

Date ___ **Monday**			
Date ___ **Tuesday**			
Date ___ **Wednesday**			
Date ___ **Thursday**			
Date ___ **Friday**			

Special Events _____   Meetings _____

Dreams are necessary to life!
Anäis Nin

Date ___ Monday			
Date ___ Tuesday			
Date ___ Wednesday			
Date ___ Thursday			
Date ___ Friday			

Special Events _____   Meetings _____

Without this playing with fantasy no
creative work has ever yet come to
birth. The debt we owe to the play of
imagination is incalculable.
Carl Gustav Jung

Week of _____   Lunchroom _____   Playground _____

Date ____ **Monday**		
Date ____ **Tuesday**		
Date ____ **Wednesday**		
Date ____ **Thursday**		
Date ____ **Friday**		

Special Events _____   Meetings _____

All of us do not have equal talent, but
all of us should have an equal oppor-
tunity to develop our talents.

John F. Kennedy

Week of _____ Lunchroom _____ Playground _____

Date ___ **Monday**			
Date ___ **Tuesday**			
Date ___ **Wednesday**			
Date ___ **Thursday**			
Date ___ **Friday**			

Special Events _____   Meetings _____

Do not train children to learning by force and harshness, but direct them to it by what amuses their minds, so that you may be better able to discover with accuracy the peculiar bent of the genius of each.   Plato

Date ___ **Monday**			
Date ___ **Tuesday**			
Date ___ **Wednesday**			
Date ___ **Thursday**			
Date ___ **Friday**			

Special Events _____   Meetings _____

The first idea that the child must acquire in order to be actively disciplined, is that of the difference between good and evil; and the task of the educator lies in seeing the child does not confound good with immobility, and evil with activity. . . our aim is to discipline for activity, for work, for good, not for immobility, not for passivity, not for obedience.

Maria Montessori

Week of _____   Lunchroom _____   Playground _____

Date ____ **Monday**			
Date ____ **Tuesday**			
Date ____ **Wednesday**			
Date ____ **Thursday**			
Date ____ **Friday**			

Likely as not, the child you can do the least with will do the most to make you proud.   Mignon McLaughlin

Week of _____   Lunchroom _____   Playground _____

Date ____ **Monday**			
Date ____ **Tuesday**			
Date ____ **Wednesday**			
Date ____ **Thursday**			
Date ____ **Friday**			

Special Events _____   Meetings _____

			As teachers, we must constantly try to improve schools and we must keep working at changing and experimenting and trying until we have developed ways of reaching every child. Albert Shanker

Week of _____   Lunchroom _____   Playground _____

Date ____ **Monday**			
Date ____ **Tuesday**			
Date ____ **Wednesday**			
Date ____ **Thursday**			
Date ____ **Friday**			

Look! the massy trunks
Are cased in the pure crystal; each
light spray,
Nodding and tinkling in the heaven,
Is studded with its trembling water-
drops,
That glimmer with an amethystine
light.   William Cullen Bryant

Week of _____   Lunchroom _____   Playground _____

Date ____ **Monday**			
Date ____ **Tuesday**			
Date ____ **Wednesday**			
Date ____ **Thursday**			
Date ____ **Friday**			

Special Events _____   Meetings _____

You can do anything with children if
you only play with them.
Otto von Bismarck

Week of _____   Lunchroom _____   Playground _____

Date ____ **Monday**			
Date ____ **Tuesday**			
Date ____ **Wednesday**			
Date ____ **Thursday**			
Date ____ **Friday**			

Few things help an individual more
than to place responsibility upon him,
and to let him know that you trust him.
Booker T. Washington

Date ___ **Monday**			
Date ___ **Tuesday**			
Date ___ **Wednesday**			
Date ___ **Thursday**			
Date ___ **Friday**			

Special Events _____   Meetings _____

If we work upon marble, it will perish; if we work upon brass, time will efface it; but if we work upon immortal minds, if we imbue them with principles, with love of others, we engrave on those tablets something which will brighten all eternity.   Daniel Webster

Week of _____   Lunchroom _____   Playground _____

Date _____ **Monday**			
Date _____ **Tuesday**			
Date _____ **Wednesday**			
Date _____ **Thursday**			
Date _____ **Friday**			

Special Events _____   Meetings _____

I may safely predict that the education of the future will be inventive-minded. It will be so profoundly in the high value of the inventive or creative spirit that it will set itself to develop that spirit by all means within its power.
Harry Allen Overstreet

Week of _____   Lunchroom _____   Playground _____

Date ___ **Monday**			
Date ___ **Tuesday**			
Date ___ **Wednesday**			
Date ___ **Thursday**			
Date ___ **Friday**			

Special Events _____   Meetings _____

			It is essential that the child acquire an understanding of and a lively feeling for values. Each student must acquire a vivid sense of the beautiful and of the morally good. Albert Einstein

Date ___ **Monday**			
Date ___ **Tuesday**			
Date ___ **Wednesday**			
Date ___ **Thursday**			
Date ___ **Friday**			

When the uncapped potential of a student meets the liberating art of a teacher, a miracle unfolds.
Mary Hatwood Futrell

Week of _____   Lunchroom _____   Playground _____

Date ___ **Monday**			
Date ___ **Tuesday**			
Date ___ **Wednesday**			
Date ___ **Thursday**			
Date ___ **Friday**			

Special Events _____   Meetings _____

The aim of education should be to teach us rather how to think, than what to think—rather to improve our minds, so as to enable us to think for ourselves, than to load our memories with the thoughts of others.

James Beattie

Date ___ Monday			
Date ___ Tuesday			
Date ___ Wednesday			
Date ___ Thursday			
Date ___ Friday			

Special Events _____   Meetings _____

Don't judge each day by the harvest
you reap, but by the seeds you plant.
Robert Louis Stevenson

Week of _____ Lunchroom _____ Playground _____

Date _____ **Monday**			
Date _____ **Tuesday**			
Date _____ **Wednesday**			
Date _____ **Thursday**			
Date _____ **Friday**			

Special Events _____   Meetings _____

I say Live, Live, because of the sun,
the dream, the excitable gift.
Anne Sexton

Week of _____ Lunchroom _____ Playground _____

Date _____ **Monday**			
Date _____ **Tuesday**			
Date _____ **Wednesday**			
Date _____ **Thursday**			
Date _____ **Friday**			

The aim of education should be to convert the mind into a living fountain, and not a reservoir. That which is filled by merely pumping in, will be emptied by pumping out.

John Mitchell Mason

Week of _____ Lunchroom _____ Playground _____

Date ____ **Monday**			
Date ____ **Tuesday**			
Date ____ **Wednesday**			
Date ____ **Thursday**			
Date ____ **Friday**			

Learning is always rebellion. . . . Every
bit of new truth discovered is revolu-
tionary to what was believed before.
Margaret Lee Runbeck

Week of _____ Lunchroom _____ Playground _____

Date ___ **Monday**			
Date ___ **Tuesday**			
Date ___ **Wednesday**			
Date ___ **Thursday**			
Date ___ **Friday**			

Too often we underestimate the power of touch, a smile, a kind word, a listening ear, an honest compliment, or the smallest act of caring, all of which have the potential to turn a life around.   Leo Buscaglia

Week of _____   Lunchroom _____   Playground _____

Date ____ **Monday**			
Date ____ **Tuesday**			
Date ____ **Wednesday**			
Date ____ **Thursday**			
Date ____ **Friday**			

The plays of natural lively children are the infancy of art. Children live in a world of imagination and feeling. They invest the most insignificant object with any form they please and see in it whatever they wish to see.
Adam Oehlenschlaeger

Week of _____   Lunchroom _____   Playground _____

Date ___ **Monday**			
Date ___ **Tuesday**			
Date ___ **Wednesday**			
Date ___ **Thursday**			
Date ___ **Friday**			

Those who trust us educate us.
George Eliot

Date ____ **Monday**			
Date ____ **Tuesday**			
Date ____ **Wednesday**			
Date ____ **Thursday**			
Date ____ **Friday**			

Special Events _____   Meetings _____

Creativity is so delicate a flower that praise tends to make it bloom, while discouragement often nips it in the bud. Any of us will put out more and better ideas if our efforts are appreciated.
Alex F. Osborn

Week of _____   Lunchroom _____   Playground _____

Date ____ **Monday**			
Date ____ **Tuesday**			
Date ____ **Wednesday**			
Date ____ **Thursday**			
Date ____ **Friday**			

The potential possibilities of any child
are the most intriguing and stimulating
in all creation.   Ray L. Wilbur

Week of _____   Lunchroom _____   Playground _____

Monday Date ___			
Tuesday Date ___			
Wednesday Date ___			
Thursday Date ___			
Friday Date ___			

Special Events _____   Meetings _____

If, in instructing a child, you are vexed
with it for want of adroitness, try, if you
have never tried before, to write with
your left hand, and then remember,
that a child is all left hand.
John Frederick Boyes

Week of _____ Lunchroom _____ Playground _____

Date ___ **Monday**			
Date ___ **Tuesday**			
Date ___ **Wednesday**			
Date ___ **Thursday**			
Date ___ **Friday**			

Special Events _____   Meetings _____

There are two ways of spreading light:
to be the candle or the mirror that
reflects it.   Edith Wharton

Date ____ **Monday**			
Date ____ **Tuesday**			
Date ____ **Wednesday**			
Date ____ **Thursday**			
Date ____ **Friday**			

I beg you to stop apologizing for being
a member of the most important pro-
fession in the world.

William G. Carr

Week of _____   Lunchroom _____   Playground _____

Date ___ **Monday**			
Date ___ **Tuesday**			
Date ___ **Wednesday**			
Date ___ **Thursday**			
Date ___ **Friday**			

Special Events _____   Meetings _____

Teachers are more than any other
class the guardians of civilization.
Bertrand Russell

Week of _____   Lunchroom _____   Playground _____

Date ___ Monday			
Date ___ Tuesday			
Date ___ Wednesday			
Date ___ Thursday			
Date ___ Friday			

His own image was no longer the reflection of a clumsy dirty gray bird, ugly and offensive. He himself was a swan!   Hans Christian Andersen

Week of _____   Lunchroom _____   Playground _____

Date _____ **Monday**			
Date _____ **Tuesday**			
Date _____ **Wednesday**			
Date _____ **Thursday**			
Date _____ **Friday**			

Special Events _____   Meetings _____

That is happiness; to be dissolved into
something complete and great.
Willa Cather

Week of _____ Lunchroom _____ Playground _____

Date _____ **Monday**			
Date _____ **Tuesday**			
Date _____ **Wednesday**			
Date _____ **Thursday**			
Date _____ **Friday**			

Special Events _____   Meetings _____

To laugh often and love much; to win the respect of intelligent persons and the affection of children, to earn the approbation of honest critics; to appreciate beauty; to give of one's self, to leave the world a bit better, whether by a healthy child, a garden patch or a redeemed social condition; to have played and laughed with enthusiasm and sung with exultation; to know even one life has breathed easier because you have lived—that is to have succeeded.   Ralph Waldo Emerson